INSTEAD OF A SHRINE

Instead of a Shrine
Eiléan Ní Chuilleanáin

A collaboration between the
THE IRELAND CHAIR OF POETRY
and
UNIVERSITY COLLEGE DUBLIN PRESS
Preas Choláiste Ollscoile Bhaile Átha Cliath
2019

First published 2019
UNIVERSITY COLLEGE DUBLIN PRESS
UCD Humanities Institute
Room H103
Belfield
Dublin 4
www.ucdpress.ie

© Eiléan Ní Chuilleanáin

ISBN 978-1-910820-50-6
ISSN 2009-8065

The Poet's Chair series kindly supported by The Arts Council

CIP data available from the British Library

The right of Eiléan Ní Chuilleanáin to be identified as the
author of this work has been asserted by her

Typeset in Adobe Kepler by Ryan Shiels
Text design and setting by Lyn Davies Design
Printed in England on acid-free paper
by Antony Rowe, Chippenham, Wiltshire

Contents

FOREWORD

A collection of public lectures that range from quoting a seventeenth century poem to referencing an Agatha Christie crime novel will always capture attention. In three public lectures, delivered during her tenure as Ireland Professor of Poetry, Eiléan Ní Chuilleanáin has more than responded to Seamus Heaney's characterisation of the post as 'an honour as well as an office.'

She has fully embraced the many elements of the Ireland Chair of Poetry established in 1998 to celebrate in a lasting way Seamus's award of the Nobel Prize for Literature. The Arts Councils in Dublin and Belfast along with three universities – Queen's University Belfast, Trinity College Dublin and University College Dublin – came together to establish the Ireland Chair of Poetry Trust. It is a perfect example of lasting cross-border collaboration.

The impressive rollcall of poets who have held the Professorship now includes John Montague, Paula Meehan, Michael Longley, Nuala Ní Dhomhnaill, Paul Durcan and Harry Clifton.

During a three-year term, the holder of the Professorship works with students in the three universities while also engaging in wider public events including the delivery of an annual public lecture.

The Trustees of the Ireland Chair of Poetry in collaboration with UCD Press has committed to publication of the Professor's lectures to ensure a wider readership is challenged, confronted – and equally – entertained by the passionate words and thoughts of these respected and brilliant poets.

In her insightful public lectures, Eiléan takes readers in strikingly diverse directions, no more so than when she seeks to recognise what a poet looks like. When she explores the 'supreme art of languages', she gives us a wonderful understanding of the words the poet must craft together – in some ways, alchemy – to create a poem. And then with masterly playfulness she teases about what constitutes a poem. Most importantly, poetry – we are told – is something that 'can reach its readers across cultural and temporal and national gaps.'

With equal ambition Eiléan sets out to locate who are the readers of poetry, or as she asks, 'Who reads this stuff anyway?' The mismatch between poet and reader is a useful topic to burrow into, and in this collection this task is done so with both grace and poise. With these public lectures the Professor gives a voice to both the poet and poetry.

The Ireland Chair of Poetry is hugely pleased to be associated with this marvellous endeavour. Considerable thanks are due to UCD Press as well as the two Arts Councils and three universities. I would also like to acknowledge the work of my fellow Trustees, past and present.

Professor Kevin Rafter
Chair of the Board of Trustees, Ireland Chair of Poetry
October 2019

Pearse Hutchinson: A Poet and His Languages

Let me begin with the obvious: poetry is the supreme art of language, and all poets must think about words all the time they are working. There are so many forms this industrious consideration can take, producing the luxuriance of eloquent speech, or the lucid surface of a plain vernacular, or any of the variations in between. But the poet I want to discuss was fascinated by, can almost be defined by his fascination with – a much broader consideration of language than is suggested by any conversation about style.

There is a volume of essays on Pearse Hutchinson's work, edited by Philip Coleman and Maria Johnston (*From Findrum to Fisterra*, 2011), some of it written, unsurprisingly, by the friends who knew him well: Macdara Woods, Robert Welch, Ciarán O'Driscoll, Martín Veiga, Vincent Woods. Also myself. But even people who did not know him personally keep coming back to his fascination with all the dimensions of language, from place names to politics, to the dictionary, etymology – quite apart from his activity as a translator. Robert Welch wrote that 'he revels in the minutest instances of differentiation while also honouring the huge *organum* of language itself, which gives meaning to all the particulars. It is this attachment to language, in its broadest sense, that is everywhere at work in his writing.'(Robert Anthony Welch, 'The solar energy of Pearse Hutchinson', in Philip Coleman and Maria Johnston (eds), *From Findrum to Fisterra: Reading Pearse Hutchinson* (Dublin, 2011), pp 17–30, p. 19).

Looking at this poet, his relation to language and languages, I want to pay a tribute to him as someone who influenced me greatly as a poet and to consider the ways that influence works between poets.

I will be skipping about between the languages that Pearse Hutchinson knew, and the reasons he knew them, which were often personal. And I'll be skating around some of the more obvious subjects, because I want to make my way to some suggestions about the way poetry and languages relate to each other. So on one side I am being biographical and autobiographical, on the other trying to come to some quite general – I won't call them conclusions.

Starting with biography and my own reminiscence. I met Pearse Hutchinson just over fifty years ago, when I was a ridiculously young lecturer at Trinity, just back in Ireland from Oxford, and had recently won a poetry prize offered by the Irish Times. (For the first and only time in my life I had used a male pseudonym.) So, for a short time I perhaps had the kind of undeserved reputation enjoyed by someone new on the scene, and I had certainly more money than sense. Even though I had to work pretty hard like all young teachers, I remember having a strange feeling of leisure, perhaps because I had zero responsibilities, and it's when one has leisure that one makes friends. (Not, I think, like love.) The friendship was also helped by the fact that I had bought a small car, but much more fundamentally by Pearse's real interest in meeting and getting to know people and introducing them to his other friends. I ferried him and others around in that mini, I sat in pubs in the afternoons and extricated myself to go and give lectures and I went on writing the poetry I'd been cultivating in isolation in Oxford in this much more gregarious and often distracting society. Where would we be without distraction?

Much later I heard him refer to another friend with a car as 'one of my *chauffeuses*' and, later again, about the speed he had got to know someone, with the phrase '*brûler les étapes*'. The italicised relish of his pronunciation of the French words and his relish for the grammar, the push of the rule that turns 'chauffeur' into 'chauffeuse': it seems to me now, looking back at the friendship that lasted until his death 45 years later, that in getting to know him I was moving into a world of languages, closely connected with a world of poetry and perhaps more loosely with the musical – and I'd have to say political – world of the

1960s. And I stayed with it and found it was broader than one might think and had deeper roots.

My focus is on people and languages and the warmth of their encounter. My mother-in-law, who was a fine singer in Irish, had a great conversation with Pearse when she was in her late 70s, about how much each of them loved the genitive feminine in Irish, the way the definite article *an* morphs into *na:* 'Barr na sráide', 'Baile na hAb-hann,' I could hear how their close attention to the synovial joints of language led on to that appreciation that makes it come alive in poetry, and how that is illuminated by the difference between languages. (The same woman, when Seán Ó Tuama's edition of *Caoineadh Airt Uí Laoghaire* came out in the 1960s, bought it on her way home from work and got so excited reading it that she had to run upstairs and declaim it to *her* mother-in-law who had no Irish at all.)

My parents were living in Rome at the time I got to know Pearse, and I was also surrounded in Dublin by people on the move – to London, Barcelona, Berlin or Marrakesh, all attractive places. I was very glad to get away from the limitations of Oxford; whatever excitement was available there, apart from the library and the river, had passed me by. Looking back, I can see that there was more to be found there than I appreciated at the time, but also that what made me find it dull was the absence in those days (as far as I was concerned) of linguistic variety. It's in the remembered light of that liberation that I want to talk about Pearse, about his poetry. Not particularly about his poems in Irish, or about his translations from many languages, although I will be mentioning both of those subjects. I'd like to see if I can find a different way of talking about poets and words in the light (*partly*) of that conversation about the genitive.

The literary milieu I was introduced to in Dublin, in the 1960s, was centred on the pubs, which functioned, as much as watering-holes, as venues and listening points. Pearse was drawn into a weekly poetry and music session in Slattery's of Capel Street by his friend the accordionist Tony MacMahon. It was run to raise funds for the Anti-Apartheid movement, the cause which brought so many people together at that hopeful time. He invited other poets to read but there were several nights when he had to take the poetry slot himself, and he didn't read just his own poems in English and Irish. I remember hearing for the first time the names and the work of Wole Soyinka the Yoruba poet, of Nazim Hikmet the Turkish communist, of Pearse's friend the English poet P. J. Kavanagh, and naturally the names and the work of the Spanish and Catalan poets he had recently been translating.

Well the Slattery's gig folded as such things do, and with Leland Bardwell – whom I first met in Slattery's – and other friends, he and I found a different pub, Sinnots of South King street, and ran a poetry and music session for another few years. Pearse, when he had the price of a pint, sat in McDaid's of Harry Street, and poets from Canada or Holland or Spain would make their way there and he'd sign them up for a reading. American Blues singers, and uilleann pipers, and the pop revolutionaries Phil Lynott and Thin Lizzy, and Luke Kelly of the Dubliners would turn up too and they'd join in. This was until the rising cost of drink, the oil crises and inflation of the early 1970s and possibly a dawning awareness that there were other things one could do with poetry, made it seem time for a change. My own first book of poems, alongside collections by Macdara Woods and by Pearse himself (only his third in English after 27 years publishing poetry) came out in early 1973; maybe we were all starting to drift towards print.

It was the moment of the decline and demise of a number of literary magazines, especially in Dublin, and the start of others. In 1971 Pearse was appointed to a Gregory Fellowship at Leeds University which he held for three years. It was a godsend for him: we were still in Ireland a decade away from the notion of providing dedicated artists with some long-term support and Pearse, never a provident person, had been barely surviving on theatre reviewing, broadcasting and gifts from friends. But the Leeds appointment came to an end and he returned to Dublin no better off. We were glad to see him though, and it was then that with Macdara Woods and Leland Bardwell we founded the magazine *Cyphers,* announcing it in letters to everyone we knew: 'Poems welcome, in any language understood by the editors.' The first two issues appeared in 1975.

That hopeful appeal underlined what I had known by then for almost a decade: that Pearse walked the world in a cloud of languages and that different languages were always present to him, to his imagination and to his political and historical awareness. Leland, Macdara and I could all speak a few languages, but for Pearse the languages he knew, and the ones he just knew about, were an essential part of his sensibility.

There were probably biographical reasons for this. He was born in Glasgow in 1927, or perhaps it's better to say into a fragment of Glasgow, into an Irish Glaswegian Republican segment of a divided Scottish city. Since he moved to Dublin at the age of five it would be hard to say how much of his sense of the Irish link with Glasgow, and of Gaelic Scotland beyond, and of the Lowland Scots language, were formed in those first five years. And his strong sense of the particular dialects and traditions inside the various strands of Scottish identity: that must have been developed later. No doubt at all that he learned much of it from his parents, especially his mother who had spent her whole life in Glasgow until the move. He would have learned about his father losing his job because of his involvement with Sinn Féin, and about the shop his mother opened to sell Irish goods and her role as minder for Constance Markiewicz in hiding in Glasgow. And while his own independent involvement with Scotland no doubt came later, he knew that the family's history had also been his. But that conscious awareness of the linguistic variety of Scotland was different, was his own.

The family's move from Scotland to Ireland had followed De Valera's victory in the general election of 1932. Of course, this meant the encounter with a new language, Irish. Probably at first as part of the spread of knowledge acquired at school, where he describes himself as a 'happy swot'. Until the age of fifteen, he says, 'there was nothing I loved better than studying, especially those three languages', English, Irish and Latin. The qualification about age is deliberate: at fifteen he discovered alcohol and sex.

The Christian Brothers at Synge Street, where he went to school, were part of the cultural movement to recreate Irish education in a Gaelic and Catholic mode. He was certainly, by the time he left school, at odds with the church's dominant position, although he never became anti-religious in the strict sense; and his discovery of Irish as a living language was at that stage still partly in the future. His early poems, however, are not all in English – he was being published in English in the *Bell* at 18, and simultaneously in Irish in the *Capuchin Annual* – and when he went to UCD two years later at 20, it was to study Spanish and Italian, passports to a wider world. In the interval he'd written his first poem in translation (which has been lost) from the French of Valéry Larbaud. He says, – and I'm quoting all this from the introduction to his collected translations, *Done into English* – 'When and how I learnt French I've no idea'.

His travels began when he left the University without a degree, and presently he started on a precarious career as a translator. Sometimes this was well paid, when he worked for the International Labour Office in Geneva, working out of French and Spanish (so his French must have been pretty good); sometimes quite poorly when he did piece-work in Spain. But he spent more and more time in Spain, where he could live cheaply and where he could discover the variousness of Iberian culture. He described his first time on Spanish soil as 'in greater truth, Galician soil' and went on 'I began to sense, dimly at first, that the Madrid / Castilian / centralist slogan *España no es más que uno*', ('Spain is One and only One') mightn't be altogether true.' And in discovering the linguistic variety, the political oppression and the social freedoms of Spain in the mid-twentieth century, he was of course discovering himself and reinforcing his long-term interests.

I'll return to the languages of Iberia which with Irish played such an important role in his life as a poet. As they are (except for Basque, which he didn't know) related to each other, they are related to the other Latin languages, all of which, and their manifestations in different cultures, at one time or another, he explored. Because I was able to borrow books from Trinity I was asked over the years to look out for books by Malgache authors (from Madagascar) writing in French, or to find him a grammar of Occitan or of Rhaeto-Romansch, one of the languages of Switzerland that I'd never heard of. And I found him the poems of Valéry Larbaud, again, published under the fantasy name of 'A. O. Barnabooth'. The one he'd translated years earlier was about the Algerian town of Mers-el Kebir: French was a portal to many parts of the African world, as Spanish was to America, as Dutch was to Java – to countries he would never visit, continents of exile, of conquest, of postcolonial poets like the Malgache Rabearivelo.

The grammars I want to pause on, because they gave him a sense of penetrating a language he would never speak fluently but still relished. As did dictionaries. And single words – when I started to learn Romanian he came out with the Romanian word for God, 'Dumnezeu' and pronounced it joyfully. Although, as he remarked in one of his poems about being middle-aged, his Romanian was 'still stuck / at lesson eight'. As often with him, he'd started out on that language because of a friend, Justin O'Mahony, who had been to Romania.

Pearse's interest in Italian was well established in the early days, since he signed up for Italian and Spanish in UCD in 1949. (He had already discovered and had perhaps already exhausted the excellent French resources of the public library in Rathmines, most fortunately near his home.) He talked about having the impression it was a weaker language than Spanish until a teacher in UCD, Signora Gaidoni, read a poem by d'Annunzio. Again, it's a personal contact that makes the language real. Italian as an interest may have begun to reactivate later because Sammy Sheridan, his girlfriend and travelling companion for many years, had spent a year teaching in Milan. But his live Italian connection really took off when he collaborated with Melita Cataldi on the collection *Antica Lirica Irlandese,* Old Irish poetry translated into Italian. I talked to Melita and her husband Piero recently and they agreed that he never got far with spoken Italian. But, Piero said, 'he loved the words' and would repeat them over and over. The example he gave was '*le parlate*', a word not for dialects – he disliked the term – but for the other local languages of Italy which are side-lined by the Tuscan that is now standard Italian. It was so characteristic of him to reject the standard word 'dialect' with its relegation of regional speech to subordinate status.

Pearse left me his Italian books when he died and, as he was a persistent annotator, I can follow him through his reading. Several were given him by Melita and Piero, including a terrific anthology of twentieth-century poems in the *parlate, Le Parole di Legno*. And over several years he worked to translate Friulian, Romagnolo, Milanese, Venetian and Triestine poetry, using the standard Italian cribs, often into Irish but mainly, I think, to English. The world of Italian, a world which he'd been physically present in rarely enough, was one where he was always at the entrance, always distant, experiencing its richness but as a just-admitted outsider, catching at words. And now it's on this aspect of his writing, rather than his work as a translator, that I would like to focus.

So, to turn to a poem. One of his Italian visits was to Melita and Piero in Turin; he went on from there to Milan and in that city he looked up from a garden and saw an unknown little girl on a balcony who greeted him with a 'Ciao'. His poem about the meeting is a characteristic taking-apart of the word, the separation and articulation of the vowels so different from the Irish and English swallowing or mauling. He wrote the poem originally in Irish, and I'll quote a line or two and then go on with his own translation. It's the last poem, 'Ceol/ Music', in his collection of autotranslations, *The Soul that Kissed the Body*:

Glór
     íon
          caol
               glé
'Ciao'

A high
     thin
          clear
               voice
'Ciao'

Not too thin
the child's voice
'Ciao'
both *a* and *o*
coming through clear
a
   so clear
o

between them
no brusque pause
the two sounds
descending
both letters
a blend
      tho' separate ...

That *tho'* with the apostrophe – he was fond of typographical oddities; we'll have another one in a minute. 'A blend / tho' separate' is his version of his own Irish, '*spleách ar a chéíle:/ neamh-spleách*' which means literally 'interdependent / independent.'

Now, of course to translate is to rewrite, to reach for still more different ways of saying and, it seems also, different ways of writing. To hear a foreign language – also, we will see in a moment, in his case to read in a foreign language – is to be stimulated to consider all the languages within reach that offer themselves as tools of expression. And it seems to me that paradoxically this is even more true when it's a language one doesn't fully possess in the way Pearse certainly possessed Irish or Catalan. When the language keeps you out, keeps you on the threshold, you are scanning its externals: the strangeness of the words that is lost when you enter into full possession.

A book Melita and Piero gave him, Franco Fortini's *I poeti del Novecento*, 'Twentieth-century poets', bears his marks. Some of these are just glosses on unfamiliar words or things, like '*polenta*' for example.

Most, though, take us on unexpected leaps away from Italian, or away as it were from the subject. Thus, there's a passage where Fortini praises the poet Diego Valeri for his refusal of anthropomorphism when he's writing about nature and for his objectivity and avoidance of the tragic howl (the word for howl is *grido*). In the margin I find a note, two words, in two languages, in Spanish and Irish – '¡*ojalá*!' which means 'let's hope' or, as the dictionary says, 'expresses a strong desire' (which must come from the Arabic *Insh'Allah!*). Followed in the margin by the Irish word *ach* – meaning 'but' – which is written with the old dot over the 'c' to denote aspiration instead of the 'h' that many of his generation found an ugly piece of modernising. So, the two words in different languages confront each other. 'If only. But.'

Similarly, he writes 'béidir, ach' meaning 'maybe, but' in the margin of a passage where Fortini discusses Umberto Saba. It's about Saba's attitude to the Hitlerian campaign of extermination of the Jews. Fortini (himself born a Jew) said that Saba was unable to take in the genocide as total catastrophe, that like other members of the educated Jewish bourgeoisie he could not escape from the mindset of his background. Pearse is recording his doubts, without of course going into detail, one doesn't in marginalia, in fact that's what makes them so alive, they are dashed off under the forward pressure that demands that one go on reading, they give the person who finds them a tantalising sliver of a view of the mind absorbing new, perhaps unwelcome, ideas.

So, let me pause on these evidences of reading: a poet is reading in a language he doesn't know very well, annotating as he goes, sometimes just to explain unfamiliar words. He's reading it seems to me in the light of two of the other languages he knows much better, Castilian Spanish and Irish. The first is helpful because it's close to Italian, the second perhaps because it marks his sense of being an outsider, a critical reader. And the way he writes Irish is idiosyncratic, announcing his personal choices. The dot for the séimhiú in *ach* is perhaps there because it looks nice in his beautiful and unmistakeable script. When he writes 'béidir' – maybe – he doesn't use the standard spelling which includes an apostrophe after the b, followed by an aspirated and thus silent f: *b'fhéidir*. That makes it an abbreviation of two words, dob fhéidir, 'it may be' whereas in ordinary speech it becomes a single word. So, to recapitulate, we have a reader who is thinking in three languages at once, who is criticising the Italian critique of the Italian poet Saba, and simultaneously choosing to write his comments in Spanish and in a slightly deviant Irish.

I should say something about translation in the more usual sense, where you take an original work and attempt to create a version in another language, one that will simultaneously speak to the reader as if it were an original and convince them that an original exists and that it is at least as good as your version. Pearse made many translations of poetry, a collection of them appeared in 2003 as *Done into English*, and enough uncollected ones exist in both Irish and English to make a second volume. But they are not my subject here, I want rather to consider his views on language and languages in relation to translations, often by others.

In his last year in Leeds he selected the poems for a 'Translation Issue' of the legendary student magazine, *Poetry and Audience*, which appeared in that year, 1974. It's a fine collection, with distinguished poems and major translators – some of whom were very young then – so we have David McDuff from Swedish (but it's the Swedish of a minority community in Finland), Emyr Humphreys and Ciarán Carson from Welsh, as well as James Kirkup, Robert Chandler, Michael Hamburger, John Heath-Stubbs. The orientation of the collection is towards a consideration of languages, especially those that are overshadowed. There's a long extract from an eighteenth century Highland poet Alexander Macdonald describing a storm at sea, translated by Ian Crichton Smith; there is a three-page piece, 'The Cave of Gold', translated by Somhairle MacLéin from his own Scottish Gaelic and there are a medieval Italian poem by Cecco Angioleri and three sonnets from the Roman *parlata* of Giuseppe Gioacchino Belli, both translated into Scots, Cecco's by George Campbell Hay, Belli's by Robert Garioch. The first Belli sonnet, 'The Beasties of the Yirdlie Paradise', is about the suppression of the animals' language by Adam. Before he arrived they 'blethert awa like doctors in dispute' but Adam 'reiv'd from the beasts their word, garr'd them shut up, / sae he allane cuid speak and ay be richt'. So, both the Roman original and the Scots translation are talking about minor languages and linguistic standardisation.

Pearse was as I've said a great man for annotation. His own collections show he couldn't resist passing on interesting knowledge to the reader, often particular locutions such as '*un toro manso*' – 'a tame bull, is a bull that refuses to fight'. In the biographical notes to that issue of *Poetry and Audience* he gets a chance to praise not just Belli but the Italians' 'admirable tradition of non-centralist writing' and to point to an anthology edited by Pier Paolo Pasolini to find the originals. He notes that Campbell Hay is 'Barring William Neill the only Scottish poet who writes in all THREE of Scotland's languages'. If it sometimes seems that he is paying a compliment to his own trilingual Scottish inheritance, much more of his writing is about the wider world and its words. He's continually running up against words and expressions that one might characterise as exotic – but would one be right?

To move back to his time in Spain. A friend from that time, P. J. Kavanagh, was in many ways a quintessentially English poet in spite of his name. He met Pearse in Barcelona when he was working for the British Council and in his early autobiographical book *The Perfect Stranger* he gives an affectionate, not uncritical account of how Pearse appeared some years before I knew him. Things that remained true almost to the end: 'his walk, seen from afar, is astonishingly springy and eager – gives you the clue to the steely poet's independence under the diffidence, and to the appetite for life'. And something that remained to the very end, 'the best talker I've met, and the only one I've ever left feeling I was more intelligent than I'd thought.' But as a poet, scribbling in bars and at bus-stops, he was also a puzzle: 'I'd try to get him to correct a verse (it was easy to see I'd been to Oxford) and he'd agree, but he never did; instead he wrote another poem. His vocabulary was exotic, but not in the tourist-poet sense, if the word was right it went in, whatever language it was; Irish, Castilian, Dutch, even Javanese – I drew the line at *nasih goreng* which is Javanese fried rice and he replied by describing how delicious it was.'

Not surprisingly then, many of his poems are like the one I quoted earlier, about the encounter with the word, often the single word or the short phrase. He can insert a word or phrase in Irish into an English poem so that even the Irish-speaking reader or hearer suddenly sees it as out of place. Or he can appeal to a bilingual understanding, as when he writes about a Dublin tourist who is breaking up the ruins of a boat for firewood and quotes:

– an old man came
he shook his head and said:
'Áá, a mhac: ná bí ag briseadh báid'

He's hoping I think that the context will tell the monoglot reader or hearer what the old man must be saying. Other phrases in Irish occur in the same poem, 'Gaeltacht' and are not directly translated, but likewise framed in a context which should allow them to be understood. Or at least to be heard. A very fine poem set in Scotland, 'Achnasheen' is similarly aimed at a reader who can hear the pressures of languages pushing through each other. The personal dedication to a friend, Eoghan Ó Néill is important here. I'll quote the opening lines:

'You'd miss the Gaelic from the placenames',
you said, turning from the danger seat to me in the back swigging Talisker
driving through Wester Ross making for the Kyle of Lochalsh.
And the next signpost we came to was Achnasheen.

How could there be any Gaelic 'for' Achnasheen?
It isn't Gaelic any more. It could never be English …

The focus on one place name, Achnasheen, is aided by the other words, from the slanginess of 'danger seat' to the specificity of 'swigging' and the brand name of the whiskey, on to the actual place names, from Germanic Wester Ross, to the Kyle of Lochalsh (Gaelic words in English syntax), to the purity of the name Achnasheen. This is a poem about the obliteration of Gaelic placenames in both Ireland and Scotland, the slamming of the door on the Celtic languages, the 'maiming ugliness' in East Ulster of:

> guessing the real names, failing to guess, the irk of that,
> like a horsehair down the back.
>
> The Gaelic names beating their wings madly
> behind the mad cage of English ...

'Achnasheen' concludes with a desperate hope but also with a reference to the Calvinist condemnation of the pipes as *Maidean Dubh' an Donais*:

> And will the black sticks of the devil, Eoghan,
> ever pipe us into heaven at last –
> as one night down the torchlit street of Áth Dara –
> into a heaven of freedom to give
> things back
>   their true names?
>
> Like streets in Barcelona,
> Like Achnasheen,
> Belfast

But it's paradoxical of course, the paradox of the linguist who can simultaneously see the original names as the true ones, but also is aware of the fractures in the culture of the original which he is too honest to leave out ;and who doesn't care if that extra allusion distorts the shape of the poem in the way truth always distorts the words we find for it. And who is approaching Gaelic Scotland through the double glass of an alien tongue, English and a related but different one, Irish. Late in his life Pearse said to me that he would never refer to Scots *Gàidhlg*, because he felt both that he'd pronounce it wrong, and that he would be claiming a greater competence in the language than he in fact possessed. So, distance is important too.

Of course, his relationship with Scotland and its languages was complicated by his own history, his lost childhood. His salute to Campbell Hay which I've already mentioned is a rather looser gesture to the same subject. He's relating in 'Achnasheen' a conversation between people who are concerned with language because they know more than one, know several in fact, and because the occasion is an exchange tour of the two countries, shared between Irish-speaking and Scottish Gaelic-speaking poets, and an attempt to hold these uncannily separated and also similar experiences in a single frame.

The poem I turn to now is quite different, about a more prosaic encounter between languages, between a bar owner who speaks only Castilian and an American marine who speaks briefly in English and then disappears, leaving the poet and his friend who are drinking in the bar to explain what has been said. It happens in Barcelona where the dominant language is Catalan, but the prosperous bourgeois city has many immigrants, from Andalusia in the building trade, and in the bar trade, as he reminds us, from Leon, and they speak Castilian.

What the marine said was 'Is there nobody here?' but the English-speaking hearers understood he was looking for a woman. There's a niggling precision about the way the poet reports what the publican says in response:

> ... we were there
> we were three
> we were people
> 'Are we nobody?' he cried (though not in English) ...
> 'Are we not people?' he cried, at least three times
> (at times only the literal
> can express the imagination,
> achieve any generous truth)

The obligation to be literal and precise finally demands that the poet should repeat exactly what the publican Saturnino says, when he thinks of the women who will have to 'be kind to that unthinking boy, / the women from his town, the women from all over Spain':

'Con la gana que tienen
   las pobres mujeres!'
'With the hunger they have – those poor women'

and then the poet repeats and italicises the stressed syllables:

'Con la *ga*na que *tien*en
   las *pob*res mu*jeres*!'

It's a snippet of language, a language important in the world but in Catalonia not highly regarded, and it's also literalness, repetition as a poetic device. The intensity of the focus on the actual words is there to heighten the contrast with the casual way the American marine uses his words.

The crude expectation that his demand in English will be understood is a proxy for his other demands, the felt presence of the American sixth fleet in port a reminder of the political and military pressures, - and all of that leads up to the final reflection on the women:

   who were people
   who were many
   who were there.

This poem may describe a brief alcoholic encounter (and the low price and poor quality of the drink in Saturnino's bar is specified) but it finishes by conjuring a whole outside world and its historical moment. The exactness of detail is parallel with the precise account of language and pronunciation.

In other poems of Pearse Hutchinson's the attention is to words, names that have been lost, original names. In 'She Made her False Name Real' the speaker says '... we changed our names, not being martyrs, to the names they gave us.' He's talking about the forcible conversion of the Jews of Mallorca, and he continues:

A change of name's a trivial thing:
it only leads to centuries of bitterness.

He repeats:

> ... not being martyrs
> but only carpenters and tailors and bookbinders
> and the best cartographers in Europe,
> yes we all blessed ourselves like crazy
> except an old woman called Jaumeta
> whose surname is not recorded
> nor even her first name before the change.
> But she was imprisoned for eight days on bread-and-water –
> mild enough for our enlightened times ...

Turning to a later poem we find another reference to the fate of Europe's Jews, in the twentieth century, and to the casual anti-Semitism encountered in the Dublin pubs of the 1940s. Pearse looked rather Jewish and had been called a 'fuckin' Yid' in Dublin; but in Harlem in Holland in 1952 he meets an old man who courteously shows him the way to his train. In this poem, 'Odessa', one phrase is untranslated: the old man says, *Gij bent een Jied*. Like the poet we guess what he must mean, but recognise that for once it's not intended offensively, and in the ensuing tiny dialogue, the old man says why he thought so: 'De baard, said he: the beard'. So once again we're at the threshold of a language we don't know, that the poet knows imperfectly, reaching for meaning.

I always knew Pearse knew some Dutch because he translated poems from that language, by both Dutch and Belgian poets. He explains in his introduction to *Done into English* that he went to Holland on the invitation of an editor of a magazine, and once more he gives details, phrases, from the elementary grammar of the language that he used when he was there, mentions the twelve books that he had to keep in touch with the language, and the difficulty he had in getting any more in Dublin since the Dutch embassy refused to believe anyone would actually read in Dutch. A page later, he's again talking about the problems of learning a minority language, this time Catalan, which is banned from the bookshops – a friend manages to get hold of a decades-old grammar for him and he is on his way.

I have gone into all these details, not merely to record and salute a friend and colleague, though that is certainly part of my motive. Since Pearse died I have also become aware of some unexpected facts about the way influence works. One is that now he is gone I find myself occasionally writing in a voice that sounds to my ear a bit like his. Why wasn't it so when he was alive? Well, by the time I met him the elements of what I think of as my own influences were already, at 24, pretty well fixed. It's a surprise to me now how true that is. A prejudice in favour of fluency had been imbibed from Yeats, the injunction to articulate sweet sounds together. What I'd learned at school, from Racine or Dante or Horace, helped me to vary the movement of verse, what I'd picked up from Kavafis in translation had given me a way out through narrative, even an escape, from certain sexual and gendered stereotypes. From poetry in Irish I'd caught the potential of partial rhyme and syllable counting. Of course, Pearse knew about all of these things too, but he had chosen to write poetry that was an interrupted melody, a rough strangeness poking through the wrapping. Whereas I was somehow under contract to the English language, trying to make it flow, to be as seamless and smooth as I could manage, and burying the hints I'd got from other languages as deeply as the ideas that underlay the poems themselves.

I also felt a desire for criticism, to be told where I was doing it wrong, which life has on the whole failed to satisfy. Pearse said he liked my stuff, but his taste in reading was so wide and so greedy that this didn't tell me what way I ought to go, I was left to my own devices. It seems that influence can work that way. P. J. Kavanagh, too, was a poet quite unlike Pearse in his politics and his approach to poetry. But I find his account of their discussions of poetry especially illuminating because he is describing a talent I haven't got myself, but Pearse had. Kavanagh says:

To be perceptively kind about his work is the greatest service one writer can do for another. ... Quite simply, praise is of more practical use than pointing out the faults. In his relief at not having his work rejected outright (at that minute prepared to defend it to the point of absurdity), mollified so much that he can admit to himself that it may not be perfect after all – he is set free to criticise himself and if he's any good he'll be able to do that better, and more harshly, than anybody.

So, if you admire a poet but know you're not going to write like him, how does influence work? I think you learn from the person – Kavanagh's account makes that clear – and the work is part of the person but not the only relevant part. Watching Pearse I learned to recognise the ethical pressure inside language towards both clarity, and fairness which is part of clarity. And so, we have to acknowledge the particular freight of meaning a word in its original form carries, and on occasion allow it to bend the vehicle of the poem with its true weight. The strange word hits the reader like a strange idea – a word *is an idea.*

We find ourselves in the maze of languages. At first, for a little of the way in, it's transparent. Then as we move further on inside we are surrounded, hemmed in by the increasingly hairy outer shells of words that we recognise but do not possess, and beyond that is the linguistic tangle that we will never penetrate. It's because of this that the experience of reading is so individualised and the obligations of clarity – the *clearing* of a space – so pressing. And on the other hand, we must not pretend that a subject or our understanding of it is clearer than it really is. The demands of poetry are contradictory, but that is what makes it an art. How can one make an aesthetically pleasing object out of meanings? Without urgency, what is the force of language?

I started with that collection of essays that appeared in 2011, the year before Pearse died. Ciarán O'Driscoll has an essay there on 'That small vast space', the importance of 'minute details and brief moments'. When he was no longer present, my friend changed as the dead do, the space around him changed, and I found myself writing a piece that quoted his poem on Russian revolutionaries, with its small detail of eggs and cherries given to one and immediately passed on to another. I'll end by quoting the whole of that poem:

SMALL
A word you were inclined to: 'a small plant',
'a small, old naked man';
never used in a negative sense:
the small difference intrigued you,
between a word in Catalan and its Castilian cousin;
the dense closeness, the narrow gap
distancing the genitive plural in Irish
from the nominative singular,
the narrow vastness between a broad and slender *r:*
fear, fir,
like a small woman reaching up
to stroke a tall man's muscled shoulder,
as in
'To Maria Spiridonovna on her keeping'
a small gift: eggs and cherries, in Moscow in 1921 –

and in Moscow six weeks after you died, as the metro stations
filled up with soldiers on the day before the election,
I imagined messages maybe flying home
in the small languages, in Welsh, Galician, Platt-Deutsch.
I tapped one out: 'Saighdiúirí i ngach áit.
Ní rabhadar ann ar maidin.' It bounced back.
I could see the small languages clustering
like swallows on wires but then caught like the birds
beating their wings madly against the mad cage
of the imperial tongue. I watched a woman soldier
helping a small old grandmother on to the train
beneath Stalin's huge high arches at Mayakovskaya.

A transcript of a lecture given in University College Dublin on Wednesday 26 April, 2019

[20]

'I Have My People and They Are Waiting' – Who Are the Readers of Poetry?

Who reads this stuff anyway?

That was my working title for this lecture. Every poet wonders about the readers, who are they, *where* are they, what will they understand, what will they like? Interestingly enough, non-readers or reluctant readers of poetry seem to be asking the same question. *WHO READS THIS STUFF ANYWAY?* Let me start by exploring the difference between the questioners.

At the time in one's life when poetry becomes an important activity – in other words, in youth – the whole question of how people will respond becomes very pressing. All poets have had some intense experience of reading, when the mere shape of a poem, or the floodlighting of truth through its language, seemed to take over the reading mind.

And then you find that this is an experience not everyone else has had. You start to notice the warning signs posted around the cultural hoardings. And if you're turning into a poet yourself you can see that it's not just that poetry is alien to some people, but the poet is marked as a dodgy character. In my own case, I could see the warnings spread about in the popular literature of the early twentieth century and so that is where I'm going to start. However, there are other questions I'd like to mull over as well: the historical place of poetry in modern Ireland, the ways that poets have set out to reach the reader, and also the question of how we know what the reader is doing.

Poetry exists inside a wider literary milieu. So, the reader like myself who has been surrounded by poetry all her life gets an occasional sharp reminder that brings up another unwelcome truth: poetry readers are rarer than readers of prose. Perhaps not quite so rare in this country as in certain others (since lots of people get an acquaintance with poetry when they're at school and quite a few go on being interested) but rare all the same. It's quite recently that I've begun to consider how this should be so, starting with: how true is it? And have we a sense that poetry was once a great deal more popular than it is now; and is that sense well-founded? And how do people in our culture think about poetry in general? Is there an Irish twist to that attitude? And finally, what do we know or imagine about the reader's response to the poem?

A well-regarded contemporary American poet, Ben Lerner, comes from Topeka, Kansas, and he mentions his home city repeatedly in his enticingly titled short book, *The Hatred of Poetry,* rather as if he expects the reader to accept it as an explanation for his low view of poetry's public status. His prize exhibit, and his starting point, is a three-line poem, 'Poetry', by Marianne Moore; the first line of which is 'I, too, dislike it.' He writes entertainingly about William Magonagall, perceptively about Whitman and Dickinson; he illuminates the twentieth-century American poetic from Olson to Claudia Rankine, and whizzes past Plato and Sidney and Shelley. He is trenchant in his response to cultural commentators who think there was a golden moment when the poet (who just happened to be a white male) spoke for everyone and defends Plath and Heaney from the charge of having an excessively personal voice. The analysis of the public attitude leads him to conclude that people, including those who don't actually ever read it, have an idea of what poetry ought to be, but believe the poets don't adequately achieve it. His response, while admitting that every individual poem is a provisional and skewed attempt to capture the 'utopian ideal of Poetry', is that the poet is clearing 'a space for the genuine Poem that never appears'.

I admire Lerner's analysis, but I would like to start rather lower down on the intellectual scale. If we want to think about how poetry in general is regarded by a wide public, we might start by asking, how do we recognise a poem? The technical answer based on rhyme and metre is much less influential than it used to be. Most people who think they can recognise a piece of language organised as a poem are responding to the look of the thing, to the typographical effect of line breaks that are not logically paragraphs or even grammatically sentences. But in fact, the single poem only gets us so far, and we would have to look closer to see whether what it contains in its complex of sounds and meanings is indeed poetry and not a shopping list or a catalogue of pictures. If it is a unit, it is the product of an individual voice.

Which brings us back to the characteristic of all language, that it is produced by speakers and writers, that it communicates what someone wants to say. Who is this someone? I am trying in this essay firstly to look at the *social* view of the poet and then of the reader, asking about the mismatching between the two that poets complain about, that they find frustrating, so that I can go on to examine the demands the poet makes on the reader, the faith hope and charity that are expected.

When we are brought face to face with the poet, what kind of person do we expect this to be? I remember how much I was discouraged as a teenager in the 1950s by the image in popular fiction of the poet as a weedy nonentity. Some examples of this from the period between the two world wars – the kind of book my contemporaries were reading, and that I was reading too – may illustrate the connection between the poet and the poem and the society they exist in. I won't apologise for beginning with the classic detective story. These were written as puzzles, as games played between the author and the reader that draw on the conventions and expectations of the time. They ask what are people *like*, what do they tend to do? (They were also, in Ireland of the mid-century, regarded as safe literature, unlikely to spark unwholesome thoughts in the young.)

Agatha Christie's *The Mysterious Affair at Styles* (1920) has among the suspects a minor character who has spent all his money, 'gone through every penny he ever had, publishing rotten verses in fancy bindings'. So, poetry is a loss-making activity, a distraction from the serious business of making a living. Agatha Christie's reader – since this is a crime novel – is left to speculate on whether there is any link between the weakness of being a poet and a tendency to poison your stepmother. Of course, this is part of the art of the detective story, its play with prejudice and probability. People in crime novels judge by outsides, not always correctly. An element that's mentioned here and that I'll return to later is the material one: poetry is found in books recognisable by their outsides, by austere or ornate bindings, just as the poem itself is to be recognised by its shape and its context.

But back to the person who wrote the poems. Everything is worse of course if the poet is female. In the stories of P. G. Wodehouse the term poetess arouses well-founded apprehension. There is a male poet in Wodehouse's *Leave it to Psmith* (1923) who is merely incomprehensible; but there's also a female, who has been heard to ask only too comprehensible, however rhetorical, questions. Lord Emsworth says '[she] asked me if I didn't think that it was fairies' tear-drops that made the dew. Did you ever hear such dashed nonsense?' This poetess does turn out to be a jewellery thief but as she points out herself the two roles are not incompatible: 'Just you start in joshing my poems and see how quick I'll bean you with a brick'.

My subject is the reader or hearer, who is often at odds with the poet. Once again in the immortal works of Wodehouse we may gather that many of the readers of poetry are female, and even perhaps that there is a specific female taste in poetry which in turn throws the subject matter of much modern poetry into relief and may even define it as masculine. In a story called *Honeysuckle Cottage* (1925) we have a man who is haunted, apparently, by the ghost of a romantic novelist. He's a writer of hardboiled crime stories himself and he's horrified to find himself having to read poetry aloud to a young woman who has landed on his doorstep in the classic romantic ploy of getting herself injured in an accident and becoming his very unwelcome guest:

> James had to read to her – and poetry, at that; and not the jolly, wholesome sort of poetry the boys are turning out nowadays, either – good, honest stuff about sin and gas works and decaying corpses – but the old-fashioned kind with rhymes in it, dealing almost exclusively with love.

The same distrust of the female reader, and the same unease about the subject matter of modern poetry, are raised in John Buchan's *Huntingtower* (1922), though the views of the male poet here are not wholeheartedly endorsed (any more than they are in Wodehouse, by the way). The principle character is a sensible Glasgow businessman, Dickson McCunn, who has a taste for poetry – by dead poets, notably Browning – he secretly finds Robert Burns 'rather vulgar', though as a Scotsman he can't say so. When he meets a live poet, he is taken aback to find the young man rejects Browning for his 'pretty round phrases' and 'noisy invocations', declaring that poetry 'is life itself, with the tang of the raw world in it – not a sweetmeat for middle-class *women* in parlours'. [my italics] When he lends McCunn his own book it is described as 'a slim book' and 'a small volume in grey paper boards' called 'Whorls' – 'John Heritage's book'. The poet himself declares that it ought to have been called 'Drains', because 'Drains are sheer poetry'. Dickson McCunn reads the book and is puzzled by its style and language: he is stumped by 'a phrase about "an epicene lily"' and disgusted by the poems about the trenches of World War One, 'largely compounded of oaths, and rather horrible, lingering lovingly over sights and smells which everyone is aware of, but most people contrive to forget.' Also, 'the lines don't seem to scan very well.' The novel evolves into a romantic adventure story by the end of which the modern poet is quoting Shakespeare and even Tennyson: 'And deep into the dying day / The happy princess followed him.'

So: the reader and the writer of verse can be at odds, the reader can be reluctant or critical – but the reluctant reader is already part of a conversation about poetry. Stella Gibbons's *Cold Comfort Farm* in 1932 contains another female poet – 17 years old and unpublished, the marvellously named Elfine Starkadder. The ruthless heroine of the novel tells the girl that she hasn't a chance of marrying the local squire if he or his family finds out that she writes poetry. Elfine is astonished: 'I thought poetry was enough ... if you met someone you loved, and you told them you wrote poetry, that would be enough to make them love you, too.' 'On the contrary', says her mentor, 'most young men are alarmed on hearing that a young woman writes poetry. Combined with an ill-groomed head of hair and an eccentric style of dress, such an admission is almost fatal.' However, Elfine doesn't concede the pass completely: 'I shall write it secretly, and publish it when I am fifty.' We are not told what the poems are like, and it is quite possible that they are excellent.

In fact, the writer of popular fiction may well have a sneaking fondness for modern poetry combined with some doubts about the people who write it. In Dorothy Sayers' 1930 detective novel *Strong Poison* the story is partly set in bohemian and artistic London, which is depicted as multicultural and sexually tolerant, with hints at both male and female homosexuality. An evening spent by the hero cruising the studios with a woman artist includes a visit to a Russian Bolshevik hotbed where new musical compositions are performed, songs are sung in Hungarian and a man called Boris reads poetry into the artist's ear. She tells him that 'it's the best thing he has done' but she doesn't have time to listen to it all now, and escapes from the party as fast as she can. But once she is outside, rather than dismissing the whole scene as a hotchpotch of pretentious rubbish, she assures the bemused detective whom she is guiding through the labyrinth that 'most of these people are doing very good work'. An earlier novel by Sayers, *Clouds of Witness* (1926) had a similar scene in the 'Soviet club' where poetry is again discussed as audible rather than visible; a member is overheard in conversation with a woman writer, asking her: 'Have you heard Robert Snoates recite his own verse to the tom-tom and the penny whistle?'

Let me pull some of this together. The popular novelists of the period – just over 80 years ago – were aware of the prestige of poetry as an art form, of its role in their culture and of the upheavals caused by the modern movement – but they are also resistant to its pretensions. Or they think their readers will be resistant. These writers described poetry in a number of different ways which they expected their readers to recognise. It is spoken by poets to often unwilling listeners, or it comes in a particular material, printed shape, often defined as 'slim', with a recognisable binding, almost a health warning. Heritage's *Whorls* might have been published by the Cuala Press, which had a characteristic grey and white livery. Agatha Christie mentioned a 'fancy binding' which is perhaps reminiscent of an earlier period: the 1890s – W. B. Yeats's *The Wind among the Reeds* of 1899 for example, or the Pre-Raphaelites such as, say, Dante Gabriel Rossetti's binding for Christina Rossetti's poems.

The point in these narratives is that the book announces itself as poetry and by doing so challenges the common reader. And the shock effect doesn't have to be visual. Poetry may be audible, read aloud and thus impinging on the listener's precious time. In Wodehouse it intrudes on Lord Emsworth's conversation with his gardener; in Sayers is associated with inconvenient politics. Sayers' depiction of bohemia hints at the notion of poetry as something *inflicted* on the ear, though it is the Hungarian singer who comes out with the dreaded words when he is interrupted, 'I begin all over again, from the beginning.' The habitués of the Soviet Club have no manners; the enthusiast for poetry readings with music knocks the detective's bread off his table in his energetic conversation. Poetry seems to be claiming attention and effectiveness that it's not entitled to, whether that's through Elfine's belief in its capacity to arouse love, or the modernist aesthetic faith of Sayers's Bohemia.

And of course, poetry is produced by a recognisable figure, the poet. How are we supposed to recognise this creature? And might there be such a creature as a willing *male* reader? The poet and *his* reader both seem – as we've seen – to be gendered beings. To take a less frivolous writer than the ones I've been discussing, George Orwell's

Gordon Comstock in *Keep the Aspidistra Flying* (1934) has written a poem that isn't quoted in the novel; it is called 'London Pleasures' and it ends up being destroyed. He has published a first book, a 'sneaky little foolscap octavo, price three and sixpence but now reduced to a bob.' It has sold 153 copies. Poverty and unpopularity are even worse than left-wing politics.

Orwell's poet is quite aggressively masculine. He is committed to sexual liberation, hostile to feminism which he sees as merely spoiling the fun. He loves his girlfriend Rosemary but their sexual consummation is frustrated because after overcoming her scruples he hasn't provided a condom and she's afraid to take the risk of unmarried pregnancy. He later impregnates her anyway and has to give up poetry and go back to working in advertising agency – it's at that point that he drops 'London Pleasures' down a manhole.

The novel opens with a long scene set in the bookshop where Gordon Comstock works. So, he is simultaneously poet and reader as well as the broker between poets and potential readers. He looks at the books that surround him with loathing, dismissing most recent and earlier literature out of hand, making an exception for the recently dead D. H. Lawrence and 'Joyce ... before he went off his coco-nut.' He manages even more intense hatred for the bookshop's customers. The women are snobbish or sentimental or crudely in search of vicarious sex or, worst of all, interested in feminism, so he has the pleasure of announcing 'with secret joy' that the shop hasn't got a history of the suffrage movement. Male customers include an odiously respectable man probably looking for pornography and a book-stealer – and then there are two younger men. One of these is classified as a moneyed youth who 'trips Nancifully' into the shop, declares that he *adores* poetry, but then he sneaks off to wallow in books about the Russian ballet. And then there's a single frightened genuine reader who buys Lawrence's *Collected Poems,* paying six shillings – it is a substantial book this time, not a wretchedly slim one. But he's so shy that he runs away at once: the real reader seems too slippery to catch hold of.

When Gordon Comstock meets a well-disposed editor, the other man is 'used to encouraging despondent poets' and observes 'Of course I admit this isn't a hopeful age to write poetry in.' Later when the editor is late meeting his mistress she responds to his explanation 'Poet! How much did he borrow off you?' Well, who would want to enter a profession like that? These poets are always unsuccessful, always presented at the point of failing to get beyond – or even as far as – the initial sliver of print, the miserable thin first book. They are also young and thus in various ways threatening. They may be upheld by suspect coteries who are prepared to listen to the poems being intoned, but it is clear from the language of these fictions that any sensible person would run a mile from that experience.

So, is the poet's position in Ireland or in Irish fictions different? A bit, I think. In the 1890s Yeats's *Red Hanrahan* is the romantic image of the poet brought to the life – an outcast figure but one whose vision is needed by the people who are to become a new society. And by the 1920s Yeats was not only a famous poet but a Senator in a new state he had helped to create – along with much more unworldly contemporaries like George Russell and Douglas Hyde, who was to end up as President. In the 1890s, too, Bernard Shaw wrote *Candida,* where the poet Eugene is totally incompetent in everyday life. But he turns out to be 'the stronger' of the two lovers of the married lady of the title, stronger than his rival, her husband, precisely it seems because of his poetic vision. In *A Portrait*, Stephen Dedalus, like Gordon Comstock, is a poet – but the titles of Joyce's own collections suggest a view of poetry as minor art, and the collections themselves are slim enough by comparison with his fictions.

In *Ulysses* Malachi Mulligan – Oliver Gogarty – mocks the Dun Emer Guild, forerunner of the Yeats sisters' Cuala Press: 'Printed by the weird sisters in the year of the big wind.' Mulligan is the enemy even if he's given many good lines, but there is a genuine impatience with the fetish of design. Stephen has had his phase of artistic bookmaking, 'Remember your *epiphanies* written on green oval leaves, *deeply deep,* copies to be sent if you died to all the great libraries of the world, including Alexandria?' He remains the visionary, his programme of conscience creating is intact throughout the vicissitudes and the wider contexts of *Ulysses,* and his identification as poet is an essential part of that.

But the relationship in Ireland between poet and reader is soured from the beginning of the century. Yeats wrote 'Great hatred, little room' and 'The daily spite of this unmannerly town'. He may have been thinking of colleagues who resented him, and of political opponents and competitors, but he is also alienated from readers:

All day I had looked in the face
What I had hoped 'twould be
To write for my own race
And the reality;
... no knave brought to book
Who has won a drunken cheer,
The witty man and his joke
Aimed at the commonest ear ...

For many writers, the reality of poverty, censorship and the philistinism of the new state in Ireland, from the age of Joyce to the decades of Patrick Kavanagh, had among other effects the separation between the poet and his or her most likely and most influential readers, the modestly prospering class of the educated or partly educated who do all the work of society that demands any mental effort. I'm referring to an economic separation here, but other factors too contribute to making a distance.

Kavanagh and Joyce challenge the society they come from. Are the values they challenge considered to be guarded by women? The absence of an audience for serious discussion, which Seán Ó Faoláin lamented repeatedly in the *Bell,* is echoed by Kavanagh in *Envoy,* but with a gendered twist. Ó Faoláin is complaining of censorship and clerical influence; Kavanagh is raging at the lack of an ideal reader for poetry, one who would be happy to take what he calls the 'passive feminine role'. His definition and his demand bring us back to the gendering of the reader as an idealised feminine, one who is happy to receive and not to create: 'The only intelligent men ... are the women, that is the women who neither write, act, paint nor play music.'

Kavanagh's misogyny as critic is not news, nor is his talent for anger. His rage is endorsed by the editor of *Envoy*, John Ryan. There's a repeated trope in Ireland during the mid-twentieth century, the closing-down editorial, and Ryan's farewell is celebratory. He lists among the achievements of *Envoy* that: '... We afforded Patrick Kavanagh an opportunity of pouring fire and brimstone on the heads of that untalented body of poetasters who are bringing Irish writing into disrepute beyond our shores.' Actually, Kavanagh doesn't confine his assaults to poets, having plenty to say about novelists, short story writers and politicians.

But it's as a poet that he is writing, a poet who longs for that intimacy with the reader that seems only a fair return for the self-exposure that is poetry. His own closing-down editorial in *Kavanagh's Weekly* (1952) rakes all classes with grapeshot but observes, 'Our readers were many and at a pinch we might call them friends. But as a serious reading public they were not worth considering ... [they] never wrote in or showed their interest.' And the same thirst for intimacy is there in the very late *Self-Portrait*: 'The main feature about a poet ... is his humourosity. ... Beautiful women, I am glad to say, are capable of recognising the baste.'

When he talks about his 'public' there is more exposure and anxiety. The eventual title of this lecture is a misquotation of Kavanagh; the poem is called 'The Same Again':

I have my friends, my public, and they are waiting
For me to come again as their one and only bard
With a new statement that will repay all the waitment
While I was hitting the bottle hard.
I know it is not right to be light and flippant;

There are people in the streets who steer by my star.
There was nothing they could do but view me while I threw
Back large whiskeys in the corner of a smoky bar.
And if only I would get drunk it wouldn't be so bad:
With a pain in my stomach I wasn't even comic,
Swallowing every digestive pill to be had.
Some of my friends stayed faithful but quite a handful
Looked upon it as the end: I could quite safely be
Dismissed a dead loss in the final up toss.
He's finished and that's definitely.

I said 'self-exposure' and I don't just mean in autobiography. To write poetry and publish it is to issue that challenge that prompts a fierce scrutiny: 'Who does she think she is?', 'Why should we follow the twists and turns of her ideas?', 'Do you call that poetry?'. That is what the poet dreads.

Kavanagh is however also a reader. When he writes about the poems in schoolbooks and the verses in *Old Moore's Almanac* and quotes Longfellow in *Kavanagh's Weekly,* he is renewing a link with an older mode of reading poetry, reaching for a poetry that was genuinely popular. There was such poetry in Ireland, often connected with music – think of Moore's *Irish melodies.* I have spent a lifetime searching in vain for the patriotic songbooks I saw in my childhood, flimsy ephemera that contained ballads and recitations – very mixed in quality – but it was in one of those that I read 'Speranza', Lady Wilde's poem on the trial of the Sheares brothers in 1798:

'Tis midnight, falls the lamplight dull and sickly
On a pale and anxious crowd
Through the court and round the judges thronging thickly
With prayers none dare to speak aloud

The rest of the poem isn't as good as that dark, tense opening, but my memory of finding 'The Brothers: a scene from '98', in among the ballads like 'The wearing of the Green' and 'Rory on the Hill', is still one of recognition that here someone was aiming for something special. When she writes 'Two youths, two noble youths, stand prisoners at the bar / You can see them through the gloom', she's working on the reader's sensibilities, not appealing to a constituency that already has its mind made up.

Yes, poetry can be popular: those cheap collections proved it to me. And Patrick Kavanagh is popular to this day, though a recent quest for his best-loved work was easily headed by the song 'Raglan Road', which indeed he sang himself. But there are problems with the identification between the poet and the work. Kavanagh's insistence on his own identity and presence as a poet brings us to one of the motives for reading poetry, the perception of the poet's character and his social role. I think of Jem Casey, the Poet of the Pick in Flann O'Brien's *At Swim Two Birds*. O'Brien is writing satire of paint-stripping acidity on the tastes and prejudices of 1930s Ireland. He presents us with Dermot Trellis, an author who is determined to write a green book, a moral book, but then is drugged and victimised by the characters he has invented. Trellis is immured and never meets his public – he is the novelist. But the poet Jem Casey is a functioning character in the fiction, he has plenty to say for himself and before he appears in person he is introduced and announced with some flourishes, and his poetry is paraded to rival the medieval Irish lyrics of the reanimated Suibhne Geilt. The character, Shanahan introduces his recitation of 'THE WORKMAN'S FRIEND' 'with a leisure priest-like in character'. He intones:

When food is scarce and your larder bare
And no rashers grease your pan,
When hunger grows as your meals are rare –
A PINT OF PLAIN IS YOUR ONLY MAN

And so on. It's been established by John Foley of NUI, Galway that there was a Reverend James Casey who wrote moral poetry for the temperance movement that is at least as awful as that. But Flann O'Brien is not just writing an experiment in banality: he's pointing to the existence of a taste for banality in society, provided it comes from a politically acceptable source. Casey's poem is received ecstatically by Shanahan's hearers, and there's even more enthusiasm when the poet appears in person and favours them with his own rendering of 'A WORKIN MAN':

A WORKIN MAN, A WORKIN MAN,
HURRAY, HURRAY for a workin man
He'll navvy and sweat till he's nearly bet
The gift of god is a workin man.

But if we don't meet the poet, and the dimension of patriotic or class solidarity – community in fact – is missing, what then? Well, readers can create communities. In an older world when poetry was written for small groups of friends it circulated in manuscript. This went on for quite a while after the arrival of print technology – there was a cachet attached to the handwritten anthology of work, often by more than one poet. There's an example in the Library of Trinity College, the TCD manuscript of John Donne. This was put together over several years, perhaps originally copied from another manuscript made under Donne's own direction. But it contains several poems written after Donne's death, so whoever assembled it must have used it to collect poems that were in some sense favourites. So here we know we have an original reader who certainly read and appreciated and assembled the poems, even if we haven't got a name.

Much of the best-known poetry in Irish survived the bleak centuries between the Cromwellian conquest and the Revival through the work of scribes who copied poems and other Gaelic literature for patrons who must have been genuine readers. And the habit of copying poems didn't die out completely. The example I know best is a collection made by my mother when she was a teenager at boarding school and finding life tedious, whiling away the time. I have three thick hard-covered notebooks of hers, but they are numbered two, three and five so there must have been two others. I know that, since she copied out every word, she really read and chose and knew the poems. They are mostly in English, some in Irish, with one example in German and quite a few in French. When I read those poems in my own early teenage years they had the authority of that choice. Naturally, looking back, I'm interested in spotting her sources, many of them patriotic Irish anthologies; but I wonder where she got George Meredith. Donagh MacDonagh, then aged 23, was to publish his first book six years later; he was courting her sister in 1935 so that probably explains his poems copied that year...

None of the poems in English can match in my memory the shock of coming across Rimbaud's 'Le Dormeur du val', with its terrible ending. After describing the young man asleep in the valley for thirteen lines, the last one reads: 'Tranquille. Il a deux trous rouges au côté droit.' In English, 'tranquil. He has two red holes in his right side.' And then there's a poem, in the same notebook of 1935, that I have never seen in print, never seen alluded to – though I'm sure the Victorianists know it well – but I've never forgotten its opening since I read it first in that handwritten volume. The title is: 'High Tide on the coast of Lincolnshire (1571)'. It's by Jean Ingelow, and it begins:

The old mayor climbed the belfry tower
The ringers rang, by two, by three;
Pull if ye never pulled before
Good ringers pull your best; quoth he
Play up, play up, o Boston bells,
Play all your changes, all your swells
Play up 'The Brides of Enderby'.

The point being that that tune, 'The Brides of Enderby', is the warning of a dangerously high tide. It's a sustained piece of writing, with a wonderful description of the eygre, the tidal bore that drowns the speaker's daughter-in-law and her two children. It's also a sustained piece of reading, and of copying, six pages in the notebook, about a hundred and fifty lines. For me her handwriting was a total endorsement of a work that was totally new to me, unlike all the poetry I'd read before – a sort of breaking through a barrier.

When I was a bit older, and my younger sister was barely out of her teens and suffering from a bad case of unrequited love, she sat in my parents' flat in Rome and copied poems into an exercise book. I was interested in this and I went looking for poems she might like; several were rejected because they had proper names in them, which is a hazard with Renaissance poetry, my own speciality. But I hit the bullseye with Wyatt, 'They flee from me that sometime did me seek.' My sister Máire was a great reader, with pronounced tastes in European fiction and poetry as well as in English, and I wish I could ask her now whether any of those poems was actually helpful at that difficult moment in her youth.

These are my own experiences of readers close to me, the evidence I have that a poem can reach its reader across cultural and temporal and national gaps. And also, that the idea of the coterie reader, quite close to other readers and sometimes close to the poets as well, is not obsolete. But most poetry now is written in the hope of reaching beyond the immediate circle through print publication. The poet can try to get to grips with this unknown quantity, the reader of a book; Nuala Ní Dhomhnaill addresses him (I think it is a him) directly in *Tusa*. It is my closing example, and I am including my own translation. As translator you are faced with another problem of connection, in this case the one that holds together the small community of people who read poetry in a small language. They understand the allusions to song and proverb in the original; if you do not, let me assure you that the visible allusions to English proverb and song are put there to echo those in Irish.

In reading this poem, one should perhaps think of how the intimacy that is denied by the words of the poem is made present by the images, and consider whether what poetry is doing is actually creating that intimate immediacy which I've just said belongs to the reader who is part of the poet's network. I'm happy, with Wilde and Whitman, to contradict myself if you find it is so.

Tusa
Is tusa, pé thú féin,
an fíréan
a thabharfadh cluais le héisteacht,
b'fhéidir, do bhean inste scéil
a thug na cosa léi, ar éigean,
ó láthair an chatha.

Níor thugamair féin an samhradh linn
ná an geimhreadh.
Níor thriallamair ar bord loinge
go Meireacá ná ag lorg ár bhfortúin
le chéile i slí ar bith
ins na tíortha teo thar lear.

Nior ghaibheamair de bharr na gcnoc
ar chapall láidir álainn dubh.
Níor luíomair faoi chrann chaorthainn
is an oíche ag cur cuisne.
Ní lú mar a bhí tinte cnámh
is an adharc á séideadh ar thaobh na gréine.

Eadrainn bhí an fharraige mhór
atá brónach. Eadrainn
bhí na cnoic is na sléibhte
ná casann ar a chéile.

You are
Whoever you are, you are
The real thing, the witness
Who might lend an ear
To a woman with a story
Barely escaped with her life
From the place of battle.

Spring, the sweet spring, was not sweet for us
Nor winter neither.
We never stepped aboard a ship together
Bound for America to seek
Our fortune, we never
Shared those hot foreign lands.

We did not fly over the high hills
Riding the fine black stallion,
Or lie under the hazel branches
As the night froze about us,
No more than we lit bonfires of celebration
Or blew the horn on the mountainside.

Between us welled the ocean
Waves of grief. Between us
The mountains were forbidding
And the roads long, with no turning.

*A transcript of a lecture given in Trinity College Dublin on Thursday,
22 March, 2018.*

Instead of a Shrine: Poetry and Ritual

Over the decades I have spent thinking about writing poetry, and what it is that poetry attempts to do, I have been becoming more conscious of a parallel with ritual and a wish to explore what ritual and poetry have in common. My latest attempt to deal with the question starts from a seventeenth-century poem, one I've been thinking of recently; indeed, more than one person has drawn it to my attention in letters of condolence. It is the *Exequy* by Henry King, bishop of Chichester, on the death of his 24-year-old wife Anne. It is a splendid poem, one that I've known since I was an undergraduate, and returning to it has only increased my affection for it. King never wrote anything else as good; it's one of those pieces that shine out in anthologies and for one generation after another become part of their climate of feeling.

I want to talk a bit about this poem – and I hope to be forgiven for reverting to my academic pasture of the English seventeenth century. My first point is how the poet lets us know what he is aiming to do, how he tells us what kind of poem this is and thus what he thinks a poem can be – all of which is in the opening few lines. And then I want to pursue his assumptions about what a poem can do into later centuries – looking at poems of the nineteenth and twentieth centuries – and to ask: is his proposition true? Is it a general truth about poetry or does it just belong to the poems of a certain period and outlook? I should expand: I'm talking about what Henry King thinks a poem can be in the world, and the historical moment, in which he is alive, but also I am looking at what we may think it can be, from the point of view of our time and culture.

Henry King lived through a momentous phase of English history. He was the son of an Elizabethan bishop of London who became a bishop himself. In his father's day it seemed as if the great change in the religious culture of the country had happened, and had been absorbed, without in the end disrupting the whole state. Most people obeyed the same rules and prayed in the same churches as they had always known, even though the language and the theology had changed. And then it became clear that another even larger convulsion was on the way, that the arguments that had seemed settled were going to be reopened, and that the Church of England was in the way of being more radically reformed than many of its clergy and laity wished. The advocates of reform being an opposing clergy and laity who felt that the Protestant Reformation had never been properly finished.

On one side of the divided house were people who thought the church was in thrall to a heap of scandalous observances that recalled the Church of Rome; on the other were those to whom the small every-day rituals of the church, those vestments and gestures that had survived the purges of the previous century, seemed harmless, familiar and (above all) decent. The argument led to a civil war. Henry King lost his diocese, his library and his home, and lived almost in hiding for several years. Ritual, and in particular the bunch of rituals inherited from the Catholic Middle Ages, was the contentious issue, which brings me back to the first four lines of King's poem:

> Accept, thou shrine of my dead saint,
> Instead of Dirges this complaint
> And for sweet flowers to crown thy herse
> Receive a strew of weeping verse

In the first two lines there are twelve words (I'll come back later to lines three and four) and of those twelve, three keywords come from the recognisable medieval vocabulary of Catholics. A *shrine* preserves the relics of a *saint* and allows them to be venerated; the word *dirge* comes from the opening of a psalm that was used in the Latin office for the dead: *Dirige, Domine, deus meus, in conspectu tuo viam meam* – Psalm 5.

The first wave of the Reformation had as one of the most visible effects the destruction and looting and desecration of shrines. The veneration of saints was forbidden and – in the view of many people – funeral services became scarily plain affairs. King is bundling all of these rejected ritual traps into the opening of his poem.

So what? we may respond, this is a poet using a metaphor, as poets do; and he goes on in this poem to draw metaphors from many sources: from libraries, optics, geography, navigation, war. And anyway, some of these metaphors had already been co-opted or even parodied, shifted from a religious to an erotic context by many writers – a 'saint' can mean 'a mistress', a 'dirge' can mean any dolorous song. Isn't that kind of switching of register just *what poets do*? But there is another word in that little opening couplet that I want to draw attention to: *Instead.* I want to ask, is a poem in some way, and if so in what way, a substitute for something else? Can it be a substitute for a ritual, for an element in the culture that is proscribed or perhaps obsolete, at any rate an element that is under some kind of pressure?

King is writing as himself, as a prominent priest, at that point in his life an archdeacon and a well-known preacher, although when he wrote this poem he was not yet a bishop. All those words I've focused on gain a little extra weight from the known identity of the writer, and from his publicly assumed position on the condition of the Church. Like his friend John Donne he rejected outright the claims of the Roman Church, and like him he had no time for the party in the Church of England that wanted a more radical Reformation. Donne had made what is to me a very interesting comment on what poetry is capable of or is allowed to do. He was dismissing the Catholic approach to public prayers, in lines that occur in his *Second Anniversarie,* written while he was travelling in France, where he says it is:

... a place, where mis-deuotion frames
A thousand praiers to Saints, whose very names
The ancient Church knew not, Heauen knowes not yet,
And where, what lawes of Poetry admit,
Lawes of Religion, haue at least the same ...

It's as if Donne saw public religion and poetry in opposition, even in competition with each other. He is also saying that the rules of poetry may properly allow what ought properly *not* to be allowed in the church. And he's talking about that other church, the Church of Rome, as it bureaucratically regulates public worship. Just as in that marvellous poem 'The Canonization' he claims the right of poetry to substitute itself for the writing of both history and hymns. Donne was probably not ordained when he wrote 'The Canonization', but we know that his studies in theology and religious controversy occupied him long before his ordination. Canonisation in the Roman Church was changing and developing in his lifetime and it already involved the authorising from above of a special office and feast day for the saint. When Donne writes about his lady and their love:

> And if unfit for tomb or hearse
> Our legend be, it will be fit for verse;

he is distinguishing between a Legend, which is the life of a saint, and the sentimental story of two lovers; and he goes on to suggest that his love poems are the equivalent, the substitute if you like, for the public office for a saint's feast day, when the faithful will pray to them for favours, and invoke them:

> And by these hymns, all shall approve
> Us canonized for love;

> And thus invoke us ...

To give the stanza as a whole:

> And if unfit for tomb or hearse
> Our legend be, it will be fit for verse;
> And if no piece of chronicle we prove,
> We'll build in sonnets pretty rooms;
> As well a well-wrought urn becomes

The greatest ashes, as half-acre tombs,
  And by these hymns, all shall approve
  Us canonized for love …

So, while turning love into religion had been a popular game since the middle ages, I am finding, I think, that the parallel between the systems of poetry and religion is an especially live issue in the seventeenth century, because of the contemporary pressures, and because it involves substitution. For these poets, it sometimes seems that poetry compensates for a historical loss, a loss they cannot conscientiously deplore in the real world, but which still aches and requires comfort in the fictitious world of poetry.

I've said 'fictitious', and in saying that I don't mean to deny that there is a great deal of excellent poetry which makes no use of fiction. However, fiction is often the instrument that comes readiest to our hand as we write, sometimes even needing to be pushed aside, with an impatient refusal, saying 'no, I want to say just literally what I mean, or what I saw, or literally what I have found in my source'. Then there are moments in poetry where we are being asked to look at the literal truth, to look at it with such intensity that the light that emanates from it becomes indistinguishable from the radiance of fiction, or of myth, or of ritual. And then, even when we are drawn into that contemplation of the literal, we still know that the poet is not under any obligation to stick to that kind of realistic truth throughout, since in order to make us see the literal he may have to frame it in fiction.

To move forward in time and take an example of what we might call realism: Walt Whitman's poem, 'A sight in camp in the daybreak gray and dim' (A poem I first encountered in its translation into Irish by Pádraig de Brún. But that's another story):

A sight in camp in the daybreak gray and dim,
As from my tent I emerge so early sleepless
I walk in the cool fresh air the path near by the hospital
    tent,

Three forms I see on stretchers lying, brought out there untended
    lying,
Over each the blanket spread, ample brownish woollen blanket,
Gray and heavy blanket, folding, covering all,

Curious I halt and silent stand,
Then with light fingers I from the face of the nearest the first just
    lift the blanket;
Who are you elderly man so gaunt and grim, with well-gray'd
    hair, and flesh all sunken about the eyes?
Who are you my dear comrade?

Then to the second I step—and who are you my child and
    darling?
Who are you sweet boy with cheeks yet blooming?

Then to the third—a face nor child nor old, very calm, as of
    beautiful yellow-white ivory;
Young man I think I know you—I think this face is the face
    of the Christ himself,
Dead and divine and brother of all, and here again he lies.

I suppose it is obvious why I call this a poem that shadows a ritual but let me dwell briefly on some details. There is the negative to which ritual is a response: the bodies are 'untended' whereas we expect, it seems decent, that the bodies of the dead should be *attended*. Again, this is a poem with a poetic and a historical context that makes the neglect understandable: we are in the middle of the American Civil War and the attendants are preoccupied with the enormous task of helping the severely wounded to survive. The poet steps in, as he says in another poem in the sequence where this one appears, 'The Wound-Dresser':

I resign'd myself
To sit by the wounded and soothe them, or silently watch the dead.

Whitman in 'The Wound-Dresser' is also presenting his position as a substitute for something else, for writing militaristic poetry. 'Aroused and angry, I'd thought to beat the alarum and urge relentless war, / but soon my fingers fail'd me ...' he says. Instead, he positions himself on a cusp between the service to the living and the dead. If you can help a wounded man by sitting by him that is a service to the individual; but watching the dead, the ritual of the wake, is also an acknowledgement the needs of the greater number, the society that wants the dead to be treated in a seemly, a decent fashion. And the huge funereal sentiment of the nineteenth century, its cult of mourning, is being transformed at Whitman's moment; my undertaker friend, the poet Thomas Lynch, has told me that the major American elaboration of his own profession stems from the funerals of the Civil War.

But this poem of Whitman's is based on that *Instead*. It is not a funeral. He does not pray or shake holy water or conduct the bodies to a grave, he looks at them with an intensity of presence that is the mark of ritual. And like the three kings at the Christmas crib, traditionally assigned to the Three Ages of Man, the three bodies in that intense light become an image of the whole of humanity; and then again, the three are summed up in the figure of Christ, divine and dead. Because ritual is itself a substitution, an impersonation in which – for example – the blanket becomes an image of the tomb, three can stand for many, and one can speak on behalf of his congregation.

Ritual is a language: it needs a public that understands what is going on. It is expressive: it deals in the visible, in clothing, gestures and also timeframes, all of which are the conditions in which the human body operates. Poetry too, like all language, exists in time, deals in the before and after, as I'll be showing in a minute. Not denying that the poet can stand outside ritual to criticise it: Emily Dickinson comments on the standard symbols of mourning in the nineteenth century:

A darker Ribbon — for a Day —
A Crape upon the Hat —
And then the pretty sunshine comes —
And helps us to forget —

And she uses funeral as metaphor – famously, 'I felt a Funeral, in my Brain'. She is not talking about the psychological impact of bereavement, rather the social rituals that make it recognisable to outsiders.

If Dickinson is commenting on ritual – and many poets do that, I will be talking about some others – Whitman is achieving something different; he is assembling an original ritual, and one that is valid for this one occasion only, this singular encounter between the poet's lonely presence and the bodies of the unknown victims of a historical event. I think that as we read or hear his poem we *become* conscious of its ritual action: it's a movement from absorbing an autobiographical narrative to being aware that the poem is itself doing something. We become aware because we already know something about ritual and in this case about the customs surrounding death. We know probably, and Whitman's readers will have known, that these vary between religious and racial and political groups and so they are in some sense invented. And we don't see Whitman's respectful, inventive interrogation of the dead faces as a transgression. We know we are dealing with a poem not a witness statement under oath, and so we are not being asked to *believe* that there were three bodies or that they looked exactly as he describes. We *are* asked to concur with the poet that what he does is solemn and has a serious meaning for all who are virtually present as readers.

I don't want to spend time talking about theories of ritual, of which there are a few, but I will mention my own theory which is that a ritual is distinguished by the importance it allows to presence and to difference. To appreciate a ritual, you have to be present, to take part. Presence is saturating that Whitman poem: it's about being present, about attending, about encounter. When it comes to difference I should give a few examples. We know that the Eucharistic meal, the Holy Communion, like the Passover meal on which it is based, is different from an ordinary meal – the question asked at Passover is 'How is this night different from all other nights?' Then there's George Herbert's Eucharistic poem, 'Love' (it's the third with that title in his book, *The Temple*, with that title, and also the poem that completes that book). It is set up as a conversation between a host and an awkward guest. It ends 'So I did sit and eat', but we know that what the poem refers to is not an ordinary case of hospitality and that neither does it merely refer to the Communion service. It differs from both: it's a construction of the poet that refers to both, and to the Gospel parables about feasts and hosts and guests; but its individual existence is as a poem, and it is as such that it draws on our sense of social and religious ritual and calls on us to recognise that a poem has its own kind of difference.

Although I've talked about the religious poets of the seventeenth century, I hope that what I've said about the poem by Whitman suggests that it is possible, without belonging to an orthodoxy, to write poetry that creates rituals and reminds readers of how we respond to symbolic behaviour in so many aspects of our lives, as we do with social custom. And this brings us up against the issue of folklore and custom. A lot of bad poetry has been written about folk beliefs, especially in Ireland, but we should remember that there are good poems too. And here we arrive at poetry that is *about* rather than *instead...*

Pearse Hutchinson's 'Bright after Dark' has something to say about symbolic action, in a form that looks like a straight comparison of folk customs in three different cultures. Characteristically for him, he places the Irish custom between those of two other countries; none of the three countries is named in the poem but, again characteristically, he adds a note informing us where they are. I want to quote the second two-thirds of the poem, which are the Irish section and then one about Guatemala:

> In the second country,
> when you send a child out of the house at night,
> you must, if you wish it well,
> take, from the fire, a burnt-out cinder
> and place it on the palm of the child's hand
> to guard the child against the dangers of the dark.
> The cinder, in this good function, is called *aingeal*
> meaning angel.

In the third country,
if you take a journey at night, above all
in the black night of ebony, so good for witches to work in,
you dare not rely on fireflies for light,
for theirs is a brief, inconstant glow. What you must hope
is that someone before you has dropped grains of maize
on the ground to light your way; and you must drop
grains of maize for whoever comes after you:
for only maize can light the way on a dark light.

The idea of calling the cinder an 'angel' comes from Dinneen's Irish-English dictionary of 1927: one of the definitions given is 'a burnt-out cinder taken from the fire, sometimes given in their hands as a protection to children going out at night'.

You've noticed perhaps that the religious idea of the guardian angel has been appropriated for the cinder charm, and that both of the customs described are dependent on shared beliefs and shared concerns – you must hope that whoever passed before you knew about the maize and cared enough to scatter it. And our elders, those who went before us in the other sense, pass their customs on to the next generation. Putting the cooled, safe cinder in the child's hand to convince it that it will be safe – it is the transfer of a small knot of understanding into the future. It is specific to Irish culture, but its placing in Hutchinson's poem makes the point that this people of ours exists in a various world, on equal terms. And if we know this poet we know that the grouping of three peoples from Europe and beyond does not allow any of them to be called backward or superstitious. For all of us, darkness suggests unease, children are fragile, and cooperation and communication are important.

So is ritual about safety? Certainly in that poem the safe place is home, indoors, and the dangers to be addressed by ritual are outside. But the form of that poem, like the progression of Whitman's 'A sight in camp', tells us something else about ritual: it proceeds in defined stages. Although Hutchinson seems to be simply placing three instances of folk belief side by side, the shape of the piece creates an accumulation, something that might not have happened if his instances had been two or five, say.

'Bright after Dark' is an 'about' poem. It concentrates on the eternal present of folklore rather than the stages in time that mark ritual itself. The stages of progression are part of many rituals. Among the poems of R. S. Thomas there are titles, 'Threshold' and 'Gradual', titles which call our attention to the idea of ritual movement through space – the Gradual is a prayer 'so called from the steps of the altar'. Pearse Hutchinson's poem tells us that it is possible to carry something of home with us into the fearful and chaotic outer world. Its focus is on the threshold, the tension between the inside and outside, keeping at a distance those forces that are dangerous or perhaps unclean. Ritual, rather than taking up residence on that threshold, moves across it. So, we wash or sprinkle water as we enter a temple, a mosque or a church. Complicated ceremonial rules may decide who is allowed to enter – a theme I'll come back to. My point just now is that this has little to do with any 'spiritual' dimension. It is about physical boundaries, physical safety and bodily gestures. Involvement of the material and bodily makes ritual recognisable. If Whitman had not stressed the moving of the blanket, if the blanket had not been so palpable in its ample grey-brown, his poem would have fallen apart.

Thomas Kinsella's poem 'Ceremony' makes a point about this; it is also what I would call an 'Instead' poem, in that it describes, better perhaps *explores*, the entry into a church that is not particularly a safe area but is definitely a sacred space, a place that could hardly be more firmly distinguished from the outside, the ordinary world. It is the poet's awareness, his refusal to make anything transcendent of the experience, to go beyond the physical, that is different. The pious presences, the shadowy believers are important here because they share the place with him, also sharing a system of signs that tell us what place this is. The reader in turn is invited to share and recognise, for example, the bowl of blood that is the sanctuary lamp:

Ceremony

I am kneeling before the altar
under the bowl of blood
with the seed of living light.

I am yielding to an impulse
growing in the cold mornings
as I passed the great blank door,

and walked through the high darkness
in among the pious presences
praying among their candles,

to kneel at the marble rail
with my palms placed together
before the hidden Host.

*

It is accomplished:
I find that I am considering
the detail in the cold stone.

Awareness of the body.
The breath warm on my fingers.
My knees damp and chill.

I will return through the high dark
among the shadowy believers
to the orderly interests of the day.

I am reminded again of some poems of R.S. Thomas – very different in his perspective, since he writes as a priest, but similarly aware of a transitional moment in a church, as when a service has ended:

... I have stopped to listen,
After the few people have gone,
To the air recomposing itself
For vigil ...   *(In Church)*

The characteristic restraint and reticence of Kinsella's poem, the tightness
of its forms, the cool immediacy, call our attention to a strangeness
that can pass for ordinary until we attend to it. I want also to comment
on two phrases: 'It is accomplished' and, taking the last line first, 'the
orderly interests of the day'. In 'Ceremony', what is inside the church is
not the orderliness of a public ritual but a space to accommodate the
strange wild impulses that bring individuals inside. 'Ceremony' was
published in one of Kinsella's Peppercanister booklets, dated 2007,
whose title is *Belief and Unbelief*. I am tempted to see it as a reversal of
an early section of his other very fine poem, in memory of his father,
'The Messenger' from thirty years earlier, which itself moves in reverse.
There he recalls, not a movement towards a communal entry into a
church as in, say, Kavanagh's 'A Christmas Childhood', but being taken,
marched *out* of a church, shockingly 'in the middle of Mass past every-
body' during a sermon that offended his father because the priest was
telling people how to vote. So the disorderly, angry and offensive are
inside the building, and that earlier section of 'The Messenger' invokes
a kind of desecration, not absolutely unrelated to the iconoclasm of
the Reformation – which, if you remember, is where I started. But there
is also the same relish for the fabric of the church, the stonework, the
child watching his reflection in 'the brawn marble' and 'the round shaft
[that] went up shining / into a mouth of stone flowers.' I am discover-
ing, I think, that poems that substitute for rituals may also substitute
for other poems, and the reversals in Kinsella are a special kind of
difference.

So, 'It is accomplished' – not only a reference to the words of Christ
on the cross: something has happened in 'Ceremony', the poem itself.
The kneeling before the altar has a past and a future, works in stages.

There was the impulse to enter, then there's the exit; the sense of accomplishment is the middle, the still point. What happens comes out of a lack, a sense of distance from the received ritual that prompts the poem to emerge instead.

I can't talk about this subject without referring to the way ritual can exclude, or without speaking about the abjection that is part of exclusion. This brings us back to how we feel about the body and about buildings. Interiors and exteriors prompt us to think about the barriers that define them, and about the ceremonies to be engaged in at those barriers – covering your head, removing your shoes, washing your hands. These don't belong entirely in religious contexts either, but traditional religion offers us some of the most resonant metaphors. The Hebrew Bible has a range of instances of ritual purity and impurity, expressing a deep anxiety about the body's lack of stability; they don't refer just to the female body either, but the fertile female body in particular attracts that suspicion.

Dorothy Molloy's poem 'Cast Out' has a speaker who is probably female and an unclean antagonist, definitely female, the two bound together – one feeding the other. It is an exciting poem for me, since I still recall the pleasure and surprise I felt when it landed in the post as a submission to *Cyphers,* and the delight of seeing it in print in the magazine. The imagery from the Old Testament is about the ceremonial uncleanness of leprosy; the setting of the poem on the other hand is medieval, but its climate seems to me to be timeless: it's about an instinctive withdrawal from something that reeks of pollution:

> She circles my walled city with her clappers and her cup
> From battlement and organ-loft I throw her food to eat
> unleavened bread, goat's cheese, the flesh of swine'.

This poem draws almost gleefully on the repertoire, piling up uncleannesses and, worse, mixing the clean and unclean together:

I sprinkle her with clay, ignore her cries. I turn away
To ring the requiem bell. She joins the living dead.
At Mass I see her lean into the leper-squint, receive
From some gloved hand the sacred Host ...

It's a poem strongly exotic with its medieval imagery and its leper-squint, but it expresses a sense of visceral horror that is not antiquarian. Dorothy Molloy had access to some mental space where wild ideas we might want to dismiss to the past are alive and forceful. Frightening pressures are conjured and moulded; when the poem ends 'I wear beneath my robe her running sores', the present tense is not chosen lightly. However, I think this is what the Irish grammarians call the *present habitual*, *bím* rather than *táim*, a present that is not a fluid moment but a condition from which there is no escape. The ritual outcast and the unpolluted insider are bound together.

I think the ritual poem frees us from this stasis into a live present. If the link between poetry and ritual is worth talking about, it is in part because we do live in a present precariously founded on the past, which supplies us with our scariest images and which hands down our sense of ritual propriety and impropriety. Which also means (I repeat) that ritual exists apart from religious observance. I remember Anthony Cronin at a very cold graveside watching Seán Ó Faoláin to see when he would put his hat on – because then he could put his on too. Men hardly use their head coverings in ritual gestures anymore, but they used to in quite recent times. A ceremony – to return to King's 'Exequy' – that we have understandably lost touch with is the laying to bed of a new bride. It was a communal female ritual; Thomas More says 'the bride was brought to bed with honest women, as manner is in brides, ye wot well', and his friend that he's telling the story to nods in acceptance. The queen in Hamlet had looked forward to decking Ophelia's bride bed. And King writes in the 'Exequy':

So close the ground, and 'bout her shade
Black curtains draw: my bride is laid.

The other custom – I promised I would come back to his opening – of bringing flowers to funerals is still with us of course. Transformed by Henry King into a strew of weeping verse, the 'Exequy' ends with the consciousness of the body in the present tense:

> But hark! my pulse, like a soft drum,
> Beats my approach, tells thee I come   ...

The final proof of the body's instability is death. Another ancient ritual is the holding of funeral games, and my last example before wrapping up is from Nuala Ní Dhomhnaill's poem 'Oscailt an Tuama / Opening the Tomb'. This is a poem that is both archaic – it is quite a deliberately pagan poem – and focused on the present, both in what it explicitly says, its references to a custom said (in the poet's fiction) to be still observed, and also in its feminist demands on our understanding. The old woman who sits up in her grave, lively as ever, after a hundred years, prescribes rituals for present and future generations that, have to do with purification and celebration:

> Bhí an tuama le dúnadh arís
> Ar an dtríú lá
> Is do chuir sí in iúl dúinn go fuaimintiúil
> É a scríobadh is a scrabhadh
> Ó bhun go barr
> Is gan aon ruainne
> Salachair a fhágaint ann.

We would have to close the tomb / on the third day / and she gave us all our orders / to scrub it and polish it / Top to bottom / and to leave no speck / of dirt or dust in it.

> Is do chomhlíonamar na horduithe
> A leag sí síos dúinn –

suí ar thulach,
trí gáir mhaíte a ardú …
a cluichí caointe a reachtáil
gach bliain anuas
go dtí an lá inniu féin.
'Cluichí Caointe na Mór-Máthar
a thugtar orthu san riamh ó shin
agus is i Mí Mheán an Fhómhair
a chomórthar iad linn.

And we followed the directions / She had laid down for us: / to sit on a hill-top / To raise three shouts of praise … / To hold her funeral games / Every year afterwards/ Down to the present day. / 'The Great Mother's Funeral Games' / They are called ever since, / and it is in the month of September / they are held, with us, today.

The closing 'today' is my addition because I felt that the original words in Irish were more emphatically present-focused than their English equivalents. The presence of ritual, in the present tense, is imagined here as an ancestral secular injunction coming from a lively though not living forebear.

It seems to me that life is full of such injunctions and orders. The trouble is, we can't obey them. They are debts we cannot pay. To write poems is not to claim that we can write off those debts, but to acknowledge them. The sense of a debt being due comes in part from the multitude of unfairnesses that crowd history. If we're still breathing, and able to write, and have a subject worth writing about, how can we balance that with the awfulness of all that has happened by chance and by deliberate actions?

Poetry does not balance because if there were a balance, an equipoise, it would not need to move. Poetry is motion, it is made of language, and language exists in time, pushing its way forward through the contradictory impulses and flashes of awareness that surround us.

Its greatest resource is negation, the ability to acknowledge the contradictory yeses and nos of our experience, the registering of all that is missing. And that is what leads us on to the fabrication of a ritual in verse.

A transcript of a lecture given in Queen's University Belfast on Thursday, 28 March 2019

BIOGRAPHICAL NOTE

Born 1942 in Cork, she is an Emeritus Fellow of Trinity College, Dublin, and was Ireland Professor of Poetry (2016–19). She has published and edited academic articles and books on the literature of the English Renaissance, on translation, and on Irish writing in both Irish and English.

With her husband Macdara Woods (1942–2018), Leland Bardwell (1922–2016) and Pearse Hutchinson (1927–2012), she has been, since 1975, a founder and editor of the Irish poetry journal *Cyphers*. She continues to edit the journal with the help of Natasha Cuddington and her niece Léan Ní Chuilleanáin.

She has published nine collections of poetry over 47 years, and her *Selected Poems* appeared in 2008, published by Gallery Press in Ireland, Wake Forest University Press in America and Faber in Britain. *The Sun-Fish*, her seventh collection, was shortlisted for the T. S. Eliot Prize and won the Griffin International Prize for poetry in 2010; *The Boys of Bluehill* was published in 2015 by Gallery Press, and was shortlisted for the Forward Prize, the *Irish Times* Poetry Now Award and the Pigott Prize at the Listowel Writers' Week. *Dánta Antonella Anedda*, translations from Italian to Irish, was published in May 2019 (Cois Life). *The Mother House* was published in October 2019 (Gallery Press).

She has published translations from Irish (Nuala Ní Dhomhnaill, 1990, 2000, 2016; Máire Mac an tSaoi, 2011; Doireann Ní Ghríofa, 2018), Romanian (Ileana Mălăncioiu, 2005, 2011) and from several living Italian poets, notably Maria Attanasio and Antonella Anedda.

She lives in Dublin and sometimes in Umbria.

ACKNOWLEDGEMENTS

The author and publisher gratefully acknowledge the following for permission to reprint copyright material.

Pearse Hutchinson: extracts from 'Achnasheen', 'Bright after dark', 'Gaeltacht', 'Saturnino', 'She made her false name real' in *Collected poems* (Gallery, 2002), and from 'Ceol' from *The Soul that kissed the body* (Gallery, 1990). Reprinted by kind permission of Gallery Press.

Patrick Kavanagh: 'The Same Again', from *Collected Poems of Patrick Kavanagh*, edited by Antoinette Quinn (Allen Lane, 2004). Reprinted by kind permission of the Trustees of the Estate of the late Katherine B. Kavanagh, through the Jonathan Williams Literary Agency.

Thomas Kinsella: 'Ceremony', from *Belief and Unbelief* (Peppercanister pamphlet 27; Dedalus, 2007). Reprinted by kind permission of Dedalus Press.

Eiléan Ní Chuilleanáin: 'Small', from *The Boys of Bluehill* (Gallery, 2015), and 'You are', and 'Opening the Tomb', from the Irish of Nuala Ní Dhomhnaill, from *The Water-Horse* (Gallery, 2000). Reprinted by kind permission of Gallery Press.

Nuala Ní Dhomhnaill: 'Tusa', 'Oscailt an Tuama', from *The Water-Horse* (Gallery, 2000). Reprinted by kind permission of Gallery Press.

BIBLIOGRAPHY

Collections of poetry

The Boys of Bluehill (Loughcrew: Gallery Press, 2015)

The Sun-Fish (Loughcrew: Gallery Press, 2009)

Selected Poems (Loughcrew: Gallery Press, 2008; London: Faber and Faber, 2008)

The Girl who married the Reindeer (Loughcrew: Gallery Press, 2001)

The Brazen Serpent (Loughcrew: Gallery Press, 1994)

The Magdalene Sermon (Loughcrew: Gallery Press, 1989)

The Second Voyage, revised edition (Newcastle-upon-Tyne: Bloodaxe, 1986)

The Rose-Geranium (Dublin: Gallery Press, 1981)

The Second Voyage (Dublin: Gallery Press, 1977)

Cork, a sequence with drawings by Brian Lalor (Dublin: Gallery Press, 1977)

Site of Ambush (Dublin: Gallery Press, 1975)

Acts and Monuments (Dublin: Gallery Press, 1973)

Translations of poetry

Dánta Antonella Anedda, ón iodáilis (Baile Átha Cliath: Cois Life, 2019)

Legend of the walled-up wife, from the Romanian of Ileana Mălăncioiu (Loughcrew: Gallery Press, 2011)

After the Raising of Lazarus, from the Romanian of Ileana Mălăncioiu (Cork: Munster Literature Centre, 2005)

Verbale/Minutes/Tuairisc, with Cormac Ó Cuilleanáin and Gabriel Rosenstock, from the Italian of Michele Ranchetti, (Dublin: Istituto Italiano di Cultura, 2002)

The Water Horse, with Medbh McGuckian, from the Irish of Nuala Ní Dhomhnaill, (Loughcrew: Gallery Press, 2000)